# SRA OPEN COURT READING

# Sinbad
# the Pig

**SRA**

A Division of The McGraw-Hill Companies

Columbus Ohio

**www.sra4kids.com**

*SRA/McGraw-Hill*

*A Division of The* **McGraw·Hill** *Companies*

Send all inquiries to:
SRA/McGraw-Hill
8787 Orion Place
Columbus, OH 43240-4027

ISBN 0-07-569444-1
1 2 3 4 5 6 7 8 9 DBH 05 04 03 02 01

# Sinbad Scats

Gramps and Ann have a big pig.

The pig is Sinbad.
Sinbad has bad habits.

Sinbad bumps Gramps.

Ann grabs at Sinbad.
Gramps grins.

"I got him!" says Ann.

Sinbad stops and sits back.

Ann trips on Sinbad.

Ann stamps.
Gramps grins.
Sinbad naps.

"Sinbad has bad habits!" says Ann.